Reading Essentials®
in Science
LIFE SCIENCE INVESTIGATIONS

Classifying Plants and Animals

LEWIS PARKER

PERFECTION LEARNING®

Editorial Director: Susan C. Thies
Editor: Lori A. Meyer
Design Director: Randy Messer
Book Design: Emily J. Greazel
Cover Design: Michael A. Aspengren

A special thanks to the following for his scientific review of the book:
Paul J. Pistek, Instructor of Biological Sciences,
North Iowa Area Community College, Mason City, IA

Image Credits: ©Associated Press: p. 10, ©CORBIS: p. 6; ©Michael Nicholson/CORBIS:
p. 7; ©Franco Vogt/CORBIS: p. 15; ©Eric Crichton/CORBIS: p. 18 (bottom); ©Dan
Guravich/CORBIS: p. 20 (top); ©Ken Wilson; Papilio/CORBIS: p. 28 (top); ©Anthony
Cooper; Ecoscene/CORBIS: p. 28 (bottom); ©Stephen Frink/CORBIS: p. 29; ©StockFood:
p. 16 (top)

ClipArt.com: p. 5; ©Perfection Learning Corporation: pp. 9, 11 (foreground), 12, 13;
PhotoDisc: p. 8 (foreground); Photos.com: cover, pp. 1, 3, 4, 8 (background),
11 (background); 14, 16 (bottom), 17, 18 (top), 19, 20 (bottom), 21, 22, 23, 24, 25, 26, 27

Perfection Learning® Corporation
1000 North Second Avenue, P.O. Box 500
Logan, Iowa 51546-0500.
Phone: 1-800-831-4190
Fax: 1-800-543-2745
perfectionlearning.com

1 2 3 4 5 6   PP   10 09 08 07 06 05

Paperback ISBN 0-7891-6633-x
Reinforced Library Binding ISBN 0-7569-4693-x

CONTENTS

WHAT IS CLASSIFICATION?

Have you ever tried to identify a certain kind of bird in your backyard? Do you know the differences between an anteater and an ant? How is a spruce tree different from a rosebush?

It is estimated that there are 10 million to 100 million different kinds of plants and animals on Earth. The actual number is probably closer to 13 or 14 million—most being insects and **microscopic** life-forms in tropical regions. In order to understand and study this huge number of plants and animals, it's important to classify them. Classification makes scientific study and appreciation of plants and animals a lot easier.

Classification is the arrangement of objects, ideas, or information into particular groups. The members of each group have one or more characteristics in common.

You use classification all the time. You classify when you organize the items in your desk. You classify the things in your closet by placing your shirts or sweaters together in one place and all your shoes in another. Classification makes everyday life a little simpler.

Classification in Science

The science of the classification of organisms is called *taxonomy*. The classification of plants and animals started centuries ago. Classification continues today as new kinds of plants and animals are discovered.

Classification helps scientists identify and study particular plants and animals and understand their **ancestry**. Sharks, perch, whales, and dolphins all live in water, but the first two are fish and the last two are mammals. Scientists know that both mosses and daisies are plants, but they are not in the same classification.

Early Classification

One of the earliest classifications was by Aristotle. Aristotle was a Greek scientist who lived about 2300 years ago. First, Aristotle divided everything into living and nonliving classes. A rock is nonliving, but a bird is a living thing. Aristotle went further. He based his classification of animals on opposites. He divided animals into those with blood and those without blood. Horses have blood but clams do not. Aristotle further divided animals into three groups—animals that live on land, animals that mainly live in the air, and animals that live in the sea. Finally, Aristotle arranged animals on a scale. At the top of the scale was the perfect animal—humans. At the bottom of the scale were the lowest animals—such as worms and slugs.

Aristotle

16th- and 17th-Century Classification

Classification did not stop with the ancient Greeks. In the 16th century, Andrea Cesalpino divided plants into groups. He grouped them according to the shape of their fruits and seeds. Another scientist, Pierre Belon, classified animals. He classified birds according to their habitat or their environment—birds that live in or near water, wading birds, birds of prey, birds that perch in trees, and birds that live only on land. In the 17th century, John Ray classified birds according to the shape and size of their beaks.

Classification Used Today

In the 18th century, Carolus Linnaeus developed a classification system that is still used today. He placed plants and animals that were similar into large groups called *genera*. Then he gave each plant and animal a two-word name using Latin words—like a first and last

Pierre Belon

name. This is called the scientific name, or **species** name. The first word is the "generic" grouping, or genus name. The second word describes the plant or animal species, or the "specific" name. For example, a dog is *Canis familiaris*. The word *Canis* refers to the genus that includes dogs, wolves, coyotes, and jackals. The word *familiaris* describes the species of canine that belongs to a household, or is not wild.

Examples of Linnaeus's Classification of Plants and Animals

Common Name	Genus	Species
Human	*Homo*	*Homo sapiens*
Black widow spider	*Latrodectus*	*Latrodectus mactans*
White clover	*Trifolium*	*Trifolium repens*
Black cherry	*Prunus*	*Prunus serotina*

Linnaeus developed the first really scientific method of classification. He grouped plants and animals by the particular characteristics they have in common.

Scientist of Significance

Carolus Linnaeus was a Swedish scientist. He practiced medicine and later taught at the university level. In the book *Systema naturae*, written in 1735, he explained his classification of plants, animals, and minerals. In other books he classified 4400 kinds of animals and 7700 different plants. He wrote more than 180 books, including those that described the plant life in Sweden and a classification of diseases.

2

PLANTS

When you walk through your backyard, you step on grass. You see leaves falling from the trees. You smell the roses on a bush. For dinner you eat an ear of corn and a slice of tomato. Grass, trees, rosebushes, corn, and tomatoes are all plants.

Although we may not pay close attention to them, plants are all around us. They play a huge part in our lives. In fact, our **survival** depends on plants.

Mystery Plants

There are at least 275,000 different plants that have been identified. Every year scientists discover many new plants. These plants aren't actually new. It's just that no one has found and classified them before. Most mystery plants are found in out-of-the-way places. Others are discovered close to cities and highways. It's estimated that about one-fifth of all the plants on Earth have not yet been discovered.

Defining Plants

So, just what is a plant? A plant is a living thing made up of many cells. Cells are the tiny building blocks of all living things. Each of the many cells of a plant has a stiff, supportive cell wall made of a substance called **cellulose**. Within the cells of the plant that are exposed to the Sun are structures called *chloroplasts*. Chloroplasts contain a substance called *chlorophyll* that gives a plant its green color.

Because plants make their own food, they are called *producers*. Chlorophyll in the plant cells captures sunlight. The energy of the Sun is then turned into a form of energy that the plant can use. Plants use this energy to change carbon dioxide gas and water into a sugar called *glucose*. This complete process is called *photosynthesis*. Plants use glucose as their food to live, grow, and maintain their parts—roots, stems, leaves, flowers, fruits, and seeds.

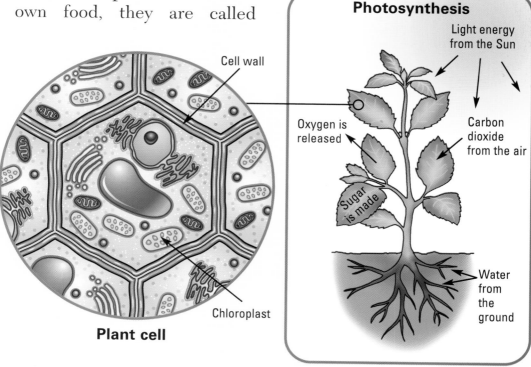

Plant cell

Cell wall

Chloroplast

Photosynthesis

Light energy from the Sun

Oxygen is released

Sugar is made

Carbon dioxide from the air

Water from the ground

Plants have a very complex life cycle. They can **reproduce** sexually or asexually. Sexual reproduction involves egg cells and sperm cells and spore formation. Asexual reproduction occurs when a piece of stem or root from a parent plant grows into a new plant.

Scientists classify plants in several ways, including by how the plant takes in water, by whether a plant produces seeds or not, and by how long a plant lives.

Technology Link

Today farmers and scientists produce many hybrid plants. A hybrid is a better plant that is created when two of the best plants are **cross-pollinated**. Hybridization is a process used to improve plants.

Planting a hybrid chestnut tree.

VASCULAR OR NONVASCULAR?

3

Plants are classified as either vascular or nonvascular. Vascular plants are able to take in water and minerals through their roots. Nonvascular plants cannot do that. Whether vascular or nonvascular, plants have an outer waxy layer called a **cuticle** that helps prevent them from drying out.

Vascular Plants

Vascular plants have tiny tubes inside them that carry water and nutrients throughout their bodies. The body of a vascular plant is made up of two parts—roots and shoots. Roots are below ground, and shoots are aboveground. Roots travel down through the soil to find moisture and minerals and to help anchor the plant in place. The roots supply water and minerals up to the shoot. The roots receive their food from the shoot above ground.

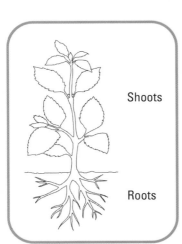

Shoots

Roots

Inside a vascular plant are two kinds of vessels—phloem and xylem. A phloem vessel carries food produced by photosynthesis. It takes the food away from the leaves and carries it to where it is needed to help the plant grow. A xylem vessel carries water and minerals absorbed by the roots from the soil up to the aboveground shoot. In this way, vascular plants receive water and nutrients from the outside.

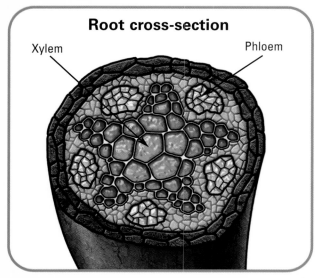

Root cross-section

Xylem

Phloem

Nonvascular Plants

When you are thirsty, you drink water. The water keeps you from becoming dehydrated. The same is true of plants. All plants have to take in, or absorb, water to survive.

Nonvascular plants do not have stems, leaves, or roots. They do not have tubes to carry food and water up and down the inside of the plant. So they absorb water right into their cells. They grow close to the ground where they can be in close contact with moisture. Being nonvascular keeps these plants very small.

Most nonvascular plants are mosses. If you take a walk in a forest, you will probably see mosses. They form patches on the ground that look like green carpet. Mosses also grow in places where other plants cannot, such as on bare, rocky cliffs or in the icy Antarctic. Most mosses, however, live in areas that are moist. This is because nonvascular plants are always in danger of drying out.

Inquire and Investigate

Question: Is a carnation a vascular or nonvascular plant?

Answer the question: I think that carnations are
_____ plants.

Form a hypothesis: A carnation is a _____ plant.

Test the hypothesis:

Materials

- ○ Measuring cup
- ○ 2 glasses
- ○ 1 white carnation with a long stem
- ○ red and blue food coloring

Procedure

Have an adult cut the stem of the carnation in half lengthwise from the bottom to about halfway up toward the flower. Pour $1/2$ cup of water into each glass. Then add enough food coloring to make the water in one glass red and the water in the other glass blue. Place the two glasses side by side. Place one half of the flower stem in the blue water and the other half in the red water. Leave the flower standing this way for four days. Observe the flower and stem for color changes.

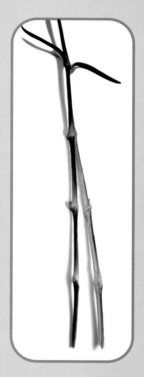

Observation: The carnation changed from white to a combination of red and blue.

Conclusion: The carnation, a flower, is a vascular plant. The colored water moved up the stem through tiny tubes called *xylem*. The colored water caused cells in the petals of the flower to change color.

Minerals in the soil are carried up the stalks of plants in this way. The minerals dissolve in water, just as the food coloring did. Then the minerals are carried to the leaves and flowers.

SEEDS OR SPORES?

Like all living things, plants must reproduce. How they reproduce is another way plants are classified. All plants reproduce by means of sex cell production and **spore** formation. These processes occur at different points in the plant life cycle.

Spores Ahoy!

Nonvascular plants and some vascular plants rely on spore formation as the main means of reproduction and plant dispersal. The spore formation, however, follows the sex cell production.

Consider a patch of moss. The sex cells—sperm and eggs—are not always on the same parts of the plant. And some moss plants produce only sperm cells and other plants produce only egg cells. When rain falls, the sperm cells swim through the drops of water to the parts of the plant where the egg cells are located. After the egg and sperm cells come together, the newly formed embryo, or baby moss, will grow into the spore-producing stage of the plant.

The spores will be produced and housed in a capsule at the end of the moss. When mature, the capsule will open up, releasing thousands of spores into the air. Only the spores that land in a moist, ideal setting will begin to grow, or germinate. The new plants will start the cycle all over again by producing egg and sperm cells.

Moss

Seeds to the Rescue

Although simple plants produce millions of spores, most spores do not grow into new plants. A plant has a much better chance of reproducing if it makes seeds.

Each seed is made up of many cells. The cells are protected with a covering. The seed contains an embryo, or baby plant, that can immediately start to grow when the conditions are right. Seeds also have a food supply. This food supply keeps the tiny plant from dying until it can exist on its own. When a new plant begins to grow, whether from a spore or a seed, the process is called *germination*.

Types of Seed Plants

There are two kinds of seed plants, and both are vascular. One group includes trees that produce seeds in cones. These plants are called *conifers*. If you look closely at a cone, you can see the seeds between the scales of the cone. Trees and shrubs such as pines, firs, redwood, and spruce are conifers. Most conifers keep their leaves year round.

Flowering plants form the other group of seed plants. In addition to their beauty, flowering plants are used for food, cloth, wood, and medicine. Many flowering plants, such as vines, trees, shrubs, and herbs, lose their leaves in the autumn. Tulips, wheat, rice, apples, corn, tomatoes, oak, and cotton are also flowering plants. Some flowering plants do not look like flowers at all. Corn is an example. Each kernel on a cob of corn is a seed. A plum is also a flowering plant. After you eat the juicy fruit, you find the stony pit inside. The seed is inside the pit.

The fruit of a flowering plant surrounds the seed and usually aids in its

Plum

dispersal. Animals may eat the fruit and **disperse** the seeds in their waste. The seeds may also be dispersed by the wind or when the fruit sticks to the fur or clothing of a passerby.

Dandelion

THE LIFE SPANS OF PLANTS

How long plants live is another factor used in classifying them. The life spans of flowering plants vary. Some plants, like sunflowers, exist for only a few months. Others, like oak trees, may grow and live for centuries.

Live It Up! (Annuals)

Plants that live during only one growing season are called *annuals*. They sprout, develop flowers and seeds, and then die within a year. Many vegetables and garden flowers like cucumbers, corn, pansies, and buttercups are annuals.

Two Good Years! (Biennials)

Biennials live for two growing seasons. For the first year, they grow and store food. During the winter they do not grow. In the second year, as spring rains appear, they produce flowers and then die. Many vegetables like carrots, potatoes, and cabbages are biennials. Farmers usually harvest these biennials before they have a chance to develop flowers and seeds. The flowers sweet William, foxglove, and primrose are other biennials.

False forget-me-nots are perennials. They belong to the genus *Brunnera*.

Live Forever! (Perennials)

The plants that live the longest are **perennials**. They produce flowers and seeds for many years. Flowering trees and shrubs are perennials. In tropical areas, perennials grow year round. In colder climates, most perennials die down to their roots or bulbs at the end of each growing season. When the rainy season begins, perennials produce new shoots and leaves.

ANIMALS

A rabbit hides from a coyote. An elephant roams across an African plain. A lobster scampers on the ocean floor. What do these creatures have in common? They are all animals.

Animals live throughout the Earth. Some animals are huge, weighing tons. Others are so small that you need a microscope to see them. What makes all these creatures animals?

Defining Animals

Animals are made up of many cells, just like plants. But the cells of animals are not stiff. Animal cells are elastic. Unlike plants, most animals have nerves and sense organs that give them information about their surroundings. These structures may help them feel, see, and smell what is near them.

Animals cannot make their own food. Animals eat plants or other animals that eat plants. This is why animals are called *consumers*.

Animals also differ from plants in the way they grow. While plants grow mainly at their tips, all parts of an animal's body grow as the animal matures.

19

Animals may be classified several ways. The easiest way to classify animals is by whether they have backbones or not. They may also be classified by the kinds of food they eat, whether they are cold-blooded or warm-blooded, and whether they produce eggs or live offspring.

Animal Traits

Most animals:

- breathe in oxygen and release carbon dioxide.
- need to eat and then use the energy from food to live and grow.
- get rid of waste that comes from eating.
- move around their environment and have movement within their bodies as well.
- have several senses—sight, hearing, smell, taste, and touch.
- continue to grow until adulthood.
- have specialized cells to do different jobs.

Black Skimmer mother bird on hatchlings and egg

Mother monkey and baby

VERTEBRATES OR INVERTEBRATES?

Bones Down the Back

Animals that have backbones are called **vertebrates.** A vertebrate has a bony skeleton inside its body called an *endoskeleton*. The skeleton grows as the animal grows. The skeleton is important because it gives the animal support. It also protects parts of the animal's body and aids in movement.

Humans are vertebrates. Put your finger at the back of your neck. Do you feel the bumps down your back? That's your backbone, or spine. An adult human has 26 vertebrae running down his or her back. They are joined like beads on a string.

There are five kinds of vertebrates—fish, amphibians, reptiles, birds, and mammals.

Fish

There are three kinds of fish. Bony fish have skeletons made of bone. They include goldfish, salmon, and trout. Another kind of fish includes sharks and rays. Their skeletons are made of a soft material called *cartilage*. The third kind of fish are jawless fish. They include the hagfish and lamprey. Some lamprey attach themselves to their prey and suck their juices out.

Amphibian—frog

Amphibians and Reptiles

Frogs, salamanders, and toads are the most common amphibians. They live part of their lives in water and part on land. Snakes, turtles, crocodiles, alligators, and lizards are reptiles. They have scales instead of fur or feathers. The scales are like tiny plates of tough material similar to your fingernails. Most reptiles swallow their food whole.

Birds

Birds are covered with feathers, can fly, and lay eggs with a hard shell. It is known that bird feathers evolved from reptilian scales.

Mammals

Mammals have hair or fur and mostly give birth to live young. They are named for the fact that they produce milk for their young. Humans, chimpanzees, gorillas, dolphins, kangaroos, and bats are examples of mammals.

Technology Link

What kind of vertebrate is it?

As **biotechnology** advances, so does our understanding about the ancestry of life. Recent recommendations to taxonomy have suggested that fish should be subdivided into five main groups and that birds should be included under reptiles.

Spineless Wonders

Animals that do not have backbones are classified as **invertebrates**. Some invertebrates have a skeleton outside their body. This skeleton is called an *exoskeleton*. It is more like a shell. As the invertebrate grows, its skeleton splits. The animal sheds its skeleton and grows a new one. Some invertebrates have no hard skeletons at all—they have soft bodies held together by fibers that are tough and strong.

Spiders, insects, centipedes, and millipedes are invertebrates. Their exoskeletons contain a substance called *chitin*. It is a stiff, hornlike material. Sponges are another kind of invertebrate. They often live at the bottom of the ocean. They attach themselves to rocks or other objects. Their skeletons are made of minerals or spongin, which is a kind of protein.

Worms make up another group of invertebrates. Their bodies are soft and slender.

Mollusks such as snails, lobsters, scallops, slugs, clams, oysters, and octopuses are also invertebrates. They have soft, boneless bodies. Mollusks' bodies are usually protected by hard shells.

Mollusk—snail

Seven Examples of Invertebrates

Invertebrate	Description or Characteristics
annelid worms	body made up of many segments
arthropods	segmented body, jointed legs, hard skeleton outside the body
cnidaria	two layers of cells with jelly in between
echinoderms	spiny skin, body divided into five sections
flatworms	worms with flat bodies
mollusks	soft body with slimy skin inside hard shell
nematodes	no segments

WHAT'S FOR DINNER?

Not all animals eat the same kinds of food. Animals can be classified as herbivores, carnivores, and omnivores.

Herbivores are animals that eat plants. Ducks, cows, horses, beavers, sloths, and locusts are all examples of herbivores. Herbivores need to consume a lot of plants to get the energy they need to live.

Horse eating grass.

Lion eating meat.

Carnivores are flesh-eating animals. They include spiders, fish, snakes, whales, dolphins, dogs, wolves, lions, and tigers. Most carnivores are hunters or scavengers.

Omnivores eat both plants and animals. They include humans, bears, raccoons, and some kinds of insects. Omnivores are not restricted to a particular food. They will eat anything that is available.

COLD-BLOODED OR WARM-BLOODED?

Animals can be classified as either cold-blooded or warm-blooded. That doesn't mean that their blood is cold or warm. It has to do with how the animal regulates its body temperature.

Warm-Blooded Animals

Only birds and mammals are warm-blooded animals. Their bodies are at a constant temperature no matter how warm or cold their surroundings might be. They generate their own heat when they are in a cooler environment. They cool themselves when their environment is hot. Warm-blooded animals often pant or sweat to cool themselves. Food is used as fuel to keep a warm-blooded animal's body temperature normal.

Humans are warm-blooded animals. A human's normal body temperature is 98.6 degrees.

Cold-Blooded Animals

Cold-blooded animals get the majority of their heat from their surroundings. They are hot when the outside temperature is hot. They are cold when they are in cold surroundings. In cold environments, cold-blooded creatures are very sluggish. Fish that live in cold winter areas move to deeper waters during the coldest months or migrate to warmer waters. Some fish have special substances in their blood that act like antifreeze to keep them from freezing even when the water freezes. Snakes, lizards, toads, frogs, salamanders, and turtles are cold-blooded animals that may hibernate during the coldest periods.

Snakes are cold-blooded animals while dogs are warm-blooded.

Asexual or Sexual?

Animals must reproduce or they will die out. Asexual reproduction occurs when animals produce offspring without having a partner. This method is used by simple animals like flatworms. It also occurs in some insects like aphids. In asexual reproduction, the offspring are clones. They are exactly like the parent. They inherit all the parent's weaknesses and strengths.

Sexual reproduction is the other way that animals reproduce. This method requires sperm and egg cells and normally involves two parents. Almost all of the world's animals use sexual reproduction.

Babies or Eggs?

As for offspring, almost all mammals produce live young rather than eggs. Then the parents may spend months or years caring for the babies. Many other vertebrates, such as most reptiles and all birds, and almost all invertebrates lay eggs.

Spiders lay a huge number of eggs. Most spiders take care of their eggs. Scorpion mothers keep the eggs inside their bodies and then give birth to live young.

Some invertebrates like lobsters release their eggs in a pocket on the underside of the mother's stomach. Female fish lay large numbers of small, soft eggs. Some sharks and certain bony fish keep their eggs in their bodies as they develop. Then they produce live offspring.

Most frogs lay long strings or large clumps of eggs numbering

Spider and babies

several hundred to a thousand. Each is coated with slippery jelly that swells when the eggs go into the water. The slimy

Frogs and frog eggs

substance doesn't taste good and keeps other creatures from eating the eggs.

An Orderly Arrangement

Classification is defined as an "orderly or systematic arrangement." As scientists classify living things, they create order in nature. As the system of classification changes and improves, new relationships among plants and animals are discovered. Classification helps us better understand our world.

Pufferfish

Technology Link

The National Center for Biotechnology Information (NCBI) was established in 1988 as a national resource for molecular biology information. The NCBI provides classification information on the Internet.

The site gives information on changes to classifications of organisms. For example, the pufferfish genus *Fugu* has recently been renamed *Takifugu*.

INTERNET CONNECTIONS AND RELATED READING FOR
Classifying Plants and Animals

http://sln.fi.edu/tfi/units/life/classify/classify.html
The Franklin Institute Online helps explain classification of plants and animals.

http://anthro.palomar.edu/animal/animal_1.htm
This tutorial site will give you more information on Carolus Linnaeus and his system of classification.

http://www.hhmi.org/coolscience/critters/index.html
This interactive site classifies critters. See if you can answer the questions and classify the animals.

http://education.leeds.ac.uk/~kh/technolo/ebp97/forest/azclass.htm
A to Z classification of both plants and animals is an informative site.

http://botit.botany.wisc.edu/courses/systematics/Phyla/Phylum_directory.html
Find out all about plant classification on this site.

Classifying Amphibians by Louise and Richard Spilsbury. Explains what amphibians are and how they are different from other animals. Heinemann, 2003. [RL 3 IL 3–5] 3453701PB 3453702CC

Classifying Birds by Louis and Richard Spilsbury. Explains what birds are and how they are classified. Heinemann, 2003. [RL 3 IL 3–5] 3453801PB 3453802CC

Classifying Mammals by Louise and Richard Spilsbury. Explains what mammals are and how they are classified. Heinemann, 2003. [RL 3 IL 3–5] 3454101PB 3454102CC

Plant Classification by Louise and Richard Spilsbury. Tells about different plants and their classification. Heinemann 2003. [RL 3 IL 3–5] 3453101PB

Plants of the Rain Forest by L. Stone. Explores types of plants found in the rain forest. Rourke Corp, 1994. [RL 3 IL K–3] 0201106HB

RL = Reading Level
IL = Interest Level
Perfection Learning's catalog numbers are included for your ordering convenience.
PB indicates paperback. HB indicates hardback. CC indicates Cover Craft.

ancestry (AN ses tree) line linking the past to the present; family history

annual (AN nyou wuhl) plant that flowers, produces seeds, and dies in one growing season

biennial (bi EN ne uhl) plant that lives for two years and produces flowers and fruit in the second year

biotechnology (bi o tek NAH luh jee) use of living things to make or improve products, plants, or animals

carnivore (KAR nuh vor) animal that eats mainly meat or other animals

cellulose (SEL you lohs) main substance of the cell walls of plants and algae

cross-pollinate (kros PAHL luh nayt) to transfer pollen from one plant to another plant

cuticle (KYOU tik uhl) thin outermost noncellular layer covering the aboveground parts of plants that help prevent water loss

disperse (di SPERS) to cause something to scatter, or go away in different directions

herbivore (HER buh vor) animal that eats mainly grass and other plants

invertebrate (in VER tuh bruht) animal that doesn't have a backbone or spine

microscopic (meye kruh SKAH pik) invisible without the use of a microscope

omnivore (AHM nuh vorz) animal that eats any kind of food, including both plants and animals

perennial (puh REN ne uhl) plant that lasts for more than two growing seasons, either dying back after each season or growing continuously

reproduce (re proh DOOS) to produce offspring

species (SPEE seez) group of similar organisms that can reproduce with each other

spore (spor) a small, usually one-celled, reproductive structure

survival (ser VEYE vuhl) continuation in life or existence

vertebrate (VER tuh bruht) animal with a backbone or a spine

31

INDEX

12233

J
570.1
PAR

Parker, Lewis.

Classifying plants
and animals

STS. JOHN AND PAUL SCHOOL